DUCKS
and other birds

Sally Morgan

Thameside Press

Distributed in the United States by
Smart Apple Media
1980 Lookout Drive
North Mankato, MN 56003

Text by Sally Morgan
Includes specialist photography by Robert Pickett

Series editor: Russell McLean
Editor: Jinny Johnson
Designer: Jacqueline Palmer
Educational consultant: Emma Harvey, Honeywell Infants School, London, U.K.

ISBN 1-930643-44-6

Printed in Hong Kong

9 8 7 6 5 4 3 2 1

Library of Congress Cataloging-in-Publication Data

Morgan, Sally.
    Ducks and other birds / written by Sally Morgan.
        p. cm. -- (Life cycles)
    ISBN 1-930643-44-6
    1. Ducks--Life cycles--Juvenile literature. 2. Birds--Life cycles--Juvenile literature.
[1. Ducks. 2. Birds.] I. Title.

QL696.A52 M67 2001
598.4'1--dc21

                                                                2001027275

Picture acknowledgements:
Ian Beames/Ecoscene: 24c. Anthony Cooper/Ecoscene: 19b, 23t. Bill Coster/NHPA:
23c. D. Ellinger/Foto Natura Stock/FLPA: 20t. Paul Ferraby/Ecoscene: 24b. M. Gore/
Ecoscene: 7t, 27b. Greenwood/Ecoscene: 27tr. Simon Grove/Ecoscene: 17t. Gryniewicz/
Ecoscene: 20b. Angela Hampton/Ecoscene: 22t. Peter Johnson/Corbis: 28t. Kintaline
Poultry & Wildfowl Centre, Benderloch, Oban, Argyll, www.domesticducks.co.uk,
+(0)1631 720223: 10t. Wayne Lawler/Ecoscene: 7c, 26t, 27tc. Papilio: f cover montage
tr, 4bl, 5c, 7b, 8t, 8b, 11t, 15br, 19tc, 19tr, 21t, 21b, 23b, 25bl, 25r, 26b, 27c. Pictor
International: b cover bl, 4tr, 29c. PowerstockZefa: 14b, 29bl. Heinz Schmidbauer/
Britstock-IFA: f cover montage br, 15cl, 24t. Pauline J. Thornton/Swift Imagery: 18b.
Roger Tidman/FLPA: 4cr. Roger Tidman/NHPA: 16br. Alan Towse/Ecoscene: 5b.
Robert A. Tyrrell/OSF: 5t, 28b. Robert Weight/Ecoscene: 17b. Whittle/Ecoscene: 22b.

All other photography by Robert Pickett.

Contents

The duck in this book is a domestic white duck, which is kept on farms around the world. Panels at the top of the pages show when each stage in the duck's life cycle takes place. The sections on a pale yellow background are about other birds, as well as other species of duck.

Words in **bold** are explained in the glossary on page 30.

Time panel

Information about other birds and ducks

What is a duck?

A duck is a type of bird. Ducks belong to a group of birds known as waterfowl because they live in and around rivers, lakes, and ponds. Swans and geese are waterfowl too.

◀ A duck has a long, wide body and short legs.

Beaks and feet

A duck's beak and feet are the perfect shape for swimming and feeding in water. Its beak is long and wide— just right for pushing into soft mud to find food.

Its large feet are **webbed**. This means that there is a flap of skin between each toe. Webbed feet help a duck to swim and to walk on mud.

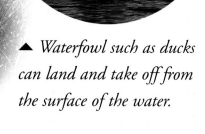

▲ Waterfowl such as ducks can land and take off from the surface of the water.

*◀ The white duck is a **domestic** bird, kept on farms.*

4

Fantastic fliers

All birds have wings, and most can fly. Bats and insects can fly too, but birds are the strongest fliers. They can reach greater heights and fly faster and for longer distances than insects or bats. Birds can **hover** in front of flowers, dive from great heights, **glide** over oceans, or dart through woodlands and forests.

▲ *The tiny bee hummingbird hovers in front of a flower by beating its wings backward and forward very fast. Then it puts its long beak into the flower to sip the sweet **nectar** inside.*

▶ *The shelduck glides over land and sea.*

▼ *The bald eagle is a hunter. It has good eyesight and a powerful beak to grip its **prey**.*

Feeding and breeding

Some birds, such as eagles, hunt and kill other animals. Other birds feed only on plants, fruits, and seeds. Some, like ducks, eat whatever they can find—plants as well as insects and small creatures. All birds lay eggs. Unlike the eggs of other animals, a bird's egg is protected by a hard shell.

Spring arrives

Many birds lay their eggs in spring. They know it's time to start egg laying when the days grow longer and warmer. But first the birds have to find partners.

▲ *A duck and a drake mate. Soon the female will lay her eggs.*

Ducks and drakes

Male ducks are called **drakes**. In spring, female ducks and drakes come together. A pair of birds stand facing each other and bob their heads up and down as part of their mating display. Soon they form a pair and **mate**. Then they begin to build a nest for their eggs.

▲ *The duck continues to lay eggs in her nest until there are about ten in all.*

A duck's nest is made up of bits of straw, dead leaves, and twigs which are collected by the female. Later, once all the eggs are laid, she may line the nest with feathers to help keep the eggs warm. She plucks these feathers from her own body. The duck lays one egg every other day until there is a **clutch** of about ten eggs.

Weaving a nest

Other birds build different kinds of
nests. The male weaver bird makes
a nest using long strips of leaves. He
starts with a single strip which he loops
and attaches to a twig. Then he loops,
twists, and knots more strips to form
a nest with a roof and an entrance.

◀ *Soft feathers from
the mother bird's
breast line the nest
of a grey teal, a type
of duck.*

▲ *A masked weaver hangs
beneath his carefully woven
nest. The nest is difficult for
enemies to reach, which helps
to keep the eggs safe.*

The swallow builds a cup-shaped nest from
mud, twigs, and grass under the **eaves** of
a roof so that the nest stays warm and dry.
A few birds do not make a nest at all. They
lay their eggs on the ground, on a branch
of a tree, or on the ledge of a cliff.

▶ *Many seabirds, such as this
tern, simply lay their eggs
on the ground.*

Birds' eggs

A bird's egg has a tough shell to protect the growing chick inside. Most birds lay eggs only for a few months each year. Chickens are bred for egg laying. Some lay one egg a day for most of the year.

▲ *The blackbird lays her beautiful blue eggs in a neat, cup-shaped nest.*

▲ *The ringed plover lays its eggs on the ground. The color and markings of the eggs make them hard to see.*

Extraordinary eggs

The largest egg is laid by the ostrich. It weighs up to 3¾ lb (1.7 kg)—as much as about 24 hen's eggs. The smallest eggs are laid by the hummingbird. These eggs are half an inch (1 cm) long and weigh a fraction of an ounce.

Some eggs are colored so that they blend with their background. Eggs laid on pebbly beaches have spotted shells which are almost impossible to see among the pebbles.

Tough shells

The shell of a duck's egg is made of a chalky substance that is surprisingly strong. Thousands of tiny holes in the shell allow air to pass from the outside into the egg, so that the developing duckling can breathe. If you crack open a duck's egg, you see a yellow egg **yolk** surrounded by a jelly-like substance that we call egg white.

Inside a duck's egg

Lying on the yolk is a tiny **embryo** which will grow into a duckling. The egg yolk is its food supply. The egg white, or **albumen**, contains the water supply for the duckling. It also helps protect it from movements and changes in temperature. The white contains a lot of **protein**, a type of food that the bird needs to grow.

▲ *The hard shell protects the contents of a duck's egg.*

▶ *A duck's egg is made up of a yellow yolk, clear egg white, and a hard shell.*

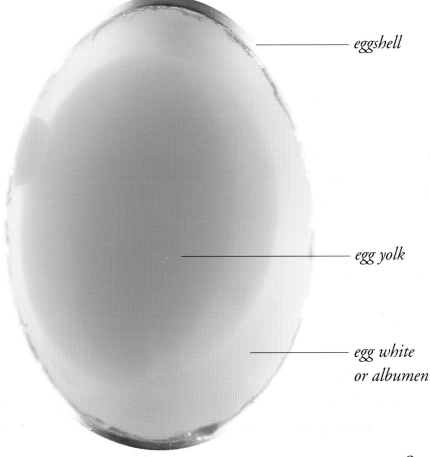

eggshell

egg yolk

egg white or albumen

9

Caring for eggs

Once the duck has laid all of her eggs, she sits on them to keep them warm. This is called incubation. Ducks **incubate** their eggs for about 28 days.

Every few hours, the duck turns the eggs so that the whole of each egg stays warm. The eggs will not develop properly if they are not kept at the right temperature all the time.

▲ *The duck sits on her eggs. She keeps them warm with the heat of her own body while they develop.*

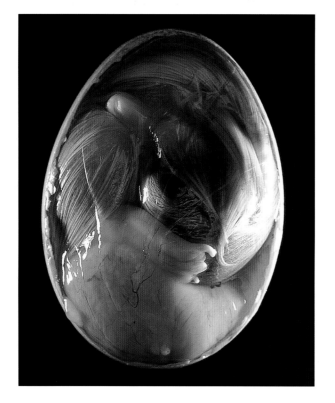

Changes inside the egg

The duckling begins life as a tiny ball of **cells** lying on the yolk. After a week or so, a network of **blood vessels** spreads out like a spider's web through the egg. These carry food and a gas called oxygen back to the growing duckling.

◀ *By 20 days the duckling is taking shape and fills more than half the egg.*

Ready to hatch

Gradually the yolk shrinks as the food is used up and the air space inside the egg becomes larger. After 28 days, the duckling has grown so large that it fills much of the egg. Its wings and legs are folded so they take up less space. Tiny peeps can be heard coming from inside the egg. The duckling is about to hatch.

▲ *This swan turns her eggs regularly during the incubation period.*

▲ *By 28 days the duckling is fully developed and ready to hatch. It has used up all of its food supply.*

Keeping eggs warm

Birds incubate their eggs for different lengths of time. The eggs of **songbirds,** such as the blue tit, hatch after just 14 days, while the swan sits on her eggs for 40 days. The brush turkey from Australia does not sit on its eggs. It makes a huge nest mound from dead leaves and soil. The female burrows into the mound and lays her eggs in the middle. The nest mound is like a compost heap. As the vegetation rots, it releases heat and keeps the eggs warm while they develop. By moving leaves and soil on and off the heap, the birds can control the temperature.

11

Time to hatch

When the duckling is ready to hatch, it has to break through the shell. The duckling has a special egg tooth on the top of its beak that it uses to force open the shell. The egg tooth looks like a tiny spike.

▲ *You can see a tiny crack in the shell near the rounded end of this egg—a sign that the duckling is about to hatch.*

▲ *The duckling has made an opening and will soon struggle out of its shell.*

Breaking out of the egg

The first sign of hatching is a crack that appears near the rounded end of the egg. This is called pipping. The duckling pushes against the shell with its egg tooth. It pokes out a tiny triangle of shell and then pecks out a circle of holes. Finally, the duckling pushes away the rounded end of the egg with its legs. The head and the wings of the duckling appear, and then the legs. It kicks away the remains of the shell.

▼ The duckling's head breaks out of the eggshell.

▼ The duckling's body appears. Now it is nearly hatched.

The duckling's feathers are wet at first. But they soon dry out and become fluffy. Its eyes are open and it can see everything around it. Its head and feet are well developed, but its wings are small. This means it cannot fly, but it can move around. All the ducklings hatch within a day of each other, so they are all the same size. They huddle under their mother for warmth and protection.

▲ The newly hatched duckling.

Following mom

Ducklings can run around within an hour of hatching. They can also see and call out to their mother.

Recognizing mother

Young ducklings can find their own food, but they cannot defend themselves. They stay close to their mother and go to her side when she calls. Ducklings learn to recognize the sound of their mother's call while they are still inside the egg. When they hatch, the first thing they see is their mother. They quickly learn her shape so they can follow her everywhere she goes. This is called **imprinting**. With the ducklings close by, parents can keep a careful watch over them and protect them from **predators**.

◀ *A mother duck checks for danger before leading her ducklings to find food.*

The parent birds need to feed, so they soon take their ducklings on their first journey to a pond or river. The ducklings trail after their parents, following the sound of their calls. When the ducklings go into the water, they stay close together in a group.

▲ *Young ducklings stay with their mother in the water. Some even ride on her back.*

A young duckling has fluffy yellow feathers called **down** feathers. These first feathers are not very **waterproof**. Young ducklings have to dry off quickly when they come out of the water, or they get cold.

Songbird chicks

The chicks of songbirds, such as the goldfinch and blackbird, are less well developed than ducklings when they hatch. The chicks are born without feathers. They are blind and helpless for the first days of their life and they stay in the nest until their feathers grow. They rely on their parents to bring them food. Once all their feathers have grown, the young birds are ready to take their first flight.

▲ *The young of this goldfinch open their beaks wide as they beg for food.*

15

Growing up

After a few weeks, a duckling's yellow feathers are replaced by white feathers. Ducklings grow quickly. They double in size almost every week for the first months of their lives.

▲ *Three weeks after hatching, a duckling has grown its first white feathers.*

Ducks have large, flat, webbed feet with toes that end in tiny claws. A duckling uses its webbed feet to paddle across the surface of the water and to dive underwater. Walking over mud is easy, as its feet do not sink into the ground.

Ducks are **omnivores**. This means that they eat both plants and animals. In fact, ducks will eat almost anything! They use their large beaks for scooping up seeds from the ground or for grabbing any slugs and snails lurking in the grass. They dabble in the mud with their beaks to find tasty food.

▲ *Six weeks after hatching, ducklings still stay close to their parents for protection.*

▶ *A duck can swim along tail-up, while it roots about for food in the water.*

16

Protective parents

Most birds have ways of keeping their young safe. Storks build huge nests high off the ground, safe from predators (right). The parents bring food back to the nest to feed their hungry chicks. On hot, sunny days, the parent birds collect water in their stomachs and empty it over their young to keep them cool.

▼ *An emperor penguin has only one chick. The chick nestles between its parent's legs, where it is kept warm by a thick fold of skin.*

Young swans are called **cygnets**. Both parents look after the cygnets. They threaten any animal that comes too close by raising their wings and hissing loudly. When their cygnets are young, one of the parents carries them around on its back.

Feathers and flying

A duck's body is covered in feathers. Birds are the only animals that have feathers. The feathers help to keep a bird warm, even in the freezing temperatures of the **Antarctic**. There are different types of feathers, each with a special job.

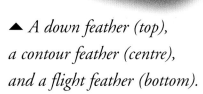

▲ *A down feather (top), a contour feather (centre), and a flight feather (bottom).*

Feathery bodies

The long, strong feathers on a duck's wings and tail are used for flying. Most of the duck's body is covered with smaller **contour** feathers, which give it a smooth outline. The smallest of all are the down feathers, which lie close to the duck's skin and keep it warm.

Caring for feathers

A duck uses its beak to nibble away any dirt from its feathers. This is called **preening**. The duck also spreads oil from a special place near its tail over its feathers to make them waterproof.

▼ *Ducks preen their feathers to keep them clean and in good condition.*

Wing shapes

Birds use their wings to fly. Birds that glide, such as the albatross, have long wings. The wings of the swift and swallow are smaller and swept back for fast flight. Ducks have more rounded wings that are good for flying short distances and ideal for making sudden changes in direction.

▶ A puffin (top) has short, round wings. A black-browed albatross (right) has long wings for gliding.

Coming in to land

Landing and taking off on water is not easy. Ducks and swans land on water by holding their wings out and putting their feet down so they skid to a halt on the surface.

To take off they have to "run on water," flapping their wings so they get enough lift to take off.

▼ Bewick's swans taking off from the water.

19

Long winter

In autumn, older ducks lose some of their old feathers and grow new ones. This is called **molting**. The new feathers are much brighter than the old ones.

▲ *A layer of fat as well as feathers keep a duck warm in winter.*

Searching for food

Winters can be long and cold. A duckling has to put on fat during the summer months when there is plenty of food to eat. During winter it has to hunt for food which may be hidden under logs or stones. Sometimes ponds and rivers freeze over, so ducks cannot dive underwater or dabble for food in the mud.

▼ *Icy winter weather can make it hard for ducks to find enough food.*

Flying to warmer parts

Many birds do not live in the same place all year round. They spend the summer in one part of the world and then fly to warmer feeding grounds in winter. This is called **migration**.

Birds such as geese and swans spend the summer in the far north. When the days grow shorter and colder they fly south to Europe, North Africa, and the southern United States. The Arctic tern may travel about 50,000 miles (80,000 km) in a year. It spends half the year in the **Arctic** and then flies to the Antarctic for the rest of the year, before returning to the Arctic.

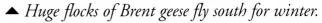

◀ *The Arctic tern makes the longest migration of any bird.*

21

Finding a partner

The young duck does not breed until it is a few years old and fully grown. Then it will have to find itself a partner, or mate.

▲ *The duck and drake perform a head-bobbing display before they start to mate.*

Some drakes and ducks have the same colored feathers. Even so, it is still possible to tell them apart. The duck has straight tail feathers while the drake has curled feathers at the end of its tail. And only the duck can quack.

Colorful feathers

Some male birds have more colorful feathers than the female of the same **species**. The males show off their feathers to the females. One of the most brilliant of all male birds is the peacock, which has long, blue-green tail feathers that he displays as a fan.

◀ *A male peacock shows off his multicolored tail feathers.*

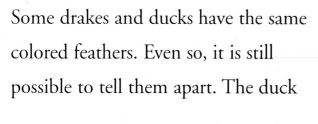

Many female birds have dull brown feathers. A female may spend weeks sitting on her eggs and dull feathers mean that she is less easily spotted by predators. This difference in appearance makes it easy to tell the male and female apart.

▶ *The male mallard (top) has colorful feathers, while the female is plainer.*

◀ *Great crested grebes perform their mating dance.*

Mating dances

Many male birds perform special dances or display their colorful feathers to attract a female. Early in the mating dance of the great crested grebe, the male and female birds face each other and move their heads from side to side.

Later, one of the birds rears up and spreads its wings while the other dives into the water. Finally, both rear up out of the water, holding pondweed in their beaks. The mandarin drake attracts a mate by displaying his bright feathers. He also makes a bubbling sound by blowing into the water.

▶ *The male mandarin shows off his feathers in a mating display.*

Life spans

Ducks live for four or five years in the wild, but in **captivity** they can live to more than 20 years. As they get older, ducks lay fewer and fewer eggs.

▲ *Domestic ducks usually live longer than wild birds.*

Many ducks are killed by predators, so few reach old age. Young ducklings may even be attacked when they are swimming. Fish, such as pike, lurk in the shadows and grab an unsuspecting duckling from below. Foxes and herons eat ducklings too.

▲ *The red fox preys on ducks and other birds.*

▼ *Farmers often keep domestic ducks in pens to protect them from predators.*

Long lives

Most small birds live for only a few years in the wild. Larger birds tend to live longer. One of the longest-living wild birds is the fulmar, a type of seabird. It can live for 50 years or more. Birds in captivity have a longer lifespan. Ostriches in zoos have lived for 60 or more years, while sulphur-crested cockatoos can reach 70 or 80. The domestic goose lives for 40 years or more.

▼ *Ostriches are the world's largest birds. In captivity, they can live for many years.*

▲ *The sulphur-crested cockatoo comes from Australia.*

All sorts of birds

There are more than 8,500 different species of birds. Some live near water, some are predators, while others have wings but cannot fly.

▲ *The emu has wings but cannot fly.*

Flightless birds

Some birds, such as the ostrich and the emu, cannot fly. They have wings, but their bodies are too heavy to lift off the ground. Another flightless bird is the kiwi. It lives in thick forests in New Zealand, where flying is difficult.

Birds of prey

Eagles and falcons are called **birds of prey**. They feed on other animals. They have powerful beaks and **talons** to catch their prey and rip it to pieces.

▼ *The peregrine falcon is a fast-flying bird of prey.*

Waterfowl

Waterfowl have beaks which are perfect for finding food in and around water. Some have straight beaks that they use to probe the mud for snails and worms. The avocet has a curved beak that it sweeps through the water to trap small animals.

▲ *The avocet has a long, curved beak.*

▲ *The macaw has a strong beak for cracking hard nuts.*

Perching birds

Perching birds are one of the largest groups. They include songbirds, such as thrushes, chickadees, and finches, that live in our gardens and parks.

▲ *The robin is a small perching bird that lives in parks, gardens, and woodlands.*

Woodland birds

Toucans, woodpeckers, parrots, and macaws all live in forests and woodland. They eat fruit, berries, and nuts.

▶ *The toucan's long beak helps it to reach fruits at the end of long branches.*

Amazing birds

- The ostrich (see page 25) is the tallest bird at about 6½ ft (2m) high. The tallest-ever ostrich stood nearly 9 ft (2.74m) high. Ostriches are too heavy to fly, but they can run as fast as 45 miles (72 km) an hour.

- The common swift can stay in the air for as long as four years. It can sleep, drink, feed, and even mate in the air. A young swift may fly 310,000 miles (500,000 km) between leaving the nest and landing two years later.

- The heaviest birds are ostriches, which weigh 275 lb (125 kg)—as much as two people. The lightest are hummingbirds (left) which can weigh as little as a sugar cube.

- The wandering albatross (right) has longer wings than any other bird. Its wings measure more than 11½ ft (3.5m) from tip to tip. Wandering albatrosses spend the year gliding over southern oceans. They feed on fish which they scoop up from the surface of the water. They only come onto land to breed.

- The whooper swan has been spotted flying at heights of about 8,000 feet (2,500m). These swans feed in the Arctic in summer and fly south to Northern Europe for the winter.

- The peregrine falcon is the fastest-flying bird. It reaches a speed of 124 miles (200 km) an hour when it swoops down to catch smaller birds in the air.

The life cycle of a duck

1 *A duck lays its eggs in a nest made of twigs and leaves.*

8 *When it is a few years old, the duck finds a partner and mates.*

2 *The egg is made up of a yellow yolk, clear egg white, and a hard shell.*

7 *After a few weeks, the yellow feathers are replaced by white ones.*

3 *The duckling feeds on the yellow egg yolk.*

6 *The duckling feeds on seeds, plants, and insects and grows quickly.*

4 *When the duckling is fully grown, it starts to peck its way out of the eggshell.*

5 *The duckling can see and run around as soon as it hatches.*

29

Glossary

albumen The clear, jelly-like substance around the yolk of an egg, also called egg white.

Antarctic The cold, polar region in the far south of the world.

Arctic The cold, polar region in the far north of the world.

bird of prey A type of bird that hunts and kills other animals. An eagle is a bird of prey.

blood vessels Tiny tubes in an animal's body and in a bird's egg that carry blood.

captivity An animal that lives in captivity is one that is kept in a zoo or as a pet.

cell A tiny unit of life from which all living things are made.

clutch A batch of eggs laid by a bird.

contour Outline or shape.

cygnet The young of a swan.

domestic Tame, or kept as a pet or for food.

down Soft feathers under a bird's main feathers. Ducks pluck out some of their down feathers to line their nests.

drake A male duck.

eaves The overhanging edge of a roof.

embryo The young of an animal in the very early stages of development.

glide Birds glide when they fly smoothly through the air without flapping their wings.

hover To remain in the air in the same spot. When hovering, a bird moves its wings backward and forward instead of up and down.

imprinting When a duckling learns to recognize the call and shape of its mother.

incubate To keep eggs warm until they hatch. Most birds keep their eggs warm by sitting on them.

mate To pair or breed.

migration A regular journey from one place to another. Migrating birds usually travel between the areas where they rear their chicks to warmer places where they spend the winter.

molt To shed old feathers and grow new ones.

nectar Sweet, sticky liquid made by flowers to attract insects. Some birds feed on nectar.

omnivore An animal that eats plants and other animals. Humans are omnivores.

perching birds A large group of birds which includes songbirds.

predator An animal that hunts and kills other animals for food.

preening When a bird nibbles its feathers with its beak to remove any dirt and to keep them in good condition.

prey Animals killed by others for food.

protein A nutrient found in food that allows the body to build new cells.

songbird A large group of birds that includes thrushes and chickadees.

species A particular type of animal that can only mate with others of the same type. Each species has its own special name.

talons The claws on a bird's feet.

waterproof Not allowing water to pass through.

webbed Having a flap of skin between each toe.

yolk The yellow food supply in an egg.

Index